AN ILLUSTRATED HISTORY OF THE
AVRO LANCASTER

AN ILLUSTRATED HISTORY OF THE
AVRO LANCASTER

MARK A. CHAMBERS

The History Press

This book is dedicated to the loving memory
of my mother, Josephine H. Chambers, who
passed away on 31 August 2023.

Front cover image: istockphoto.com/wragg
Back cover image: NARA

First published 2023

The History Press
97 St George's Place, Cheltenham,
Gloucestershire, GL50 3QB
www.thehistorypress.co.uk

British Library Cataloguing in Publication Data.
A catalogue record for this book is available from the British Library.

ISBN 978 0 7509 9465 1

Typesetting and origination by The History Press
Printed and bound in Turkey by Imak

Trees for Life

CONTENTS

Lancaster PA474 of the Battle of Britain Memorial Flight flies over British royalty in June 2013. (Carfax2 via Wikimedia Commons)

A view inside the cockpit of a Lancaster B.I, showing the pilot area and the nose section. (Paine Field USA, 2010; John Veit via Wikimedia Commons)

ACKNOWLEDGEMENTS

Numerous individuals deserve great thanks for providing crucial support for the completion of this book. First and foremost, great thanks go to my loving family – my wife Lesa and sons Patrick and Ryan – for tolerating my ceaseless words of enthusiasm and providing encouragement and support for this project. Great thanks also go to the entire staff of the Textual Reference Branch of the US National Archives and Record Administration (NARA) at College Park, Maryland; and Billy Wade and the entire staff of the Still Pictures Branch of the US NARA at College Park, Maryland. In addition, great thanks go to Amy Rigg, Commissioning Editor at The History Press, for her unwavering and fantastic encouragement and support in seeing this project through to publication.

INTRODUCTION

During the Second World War, the Avro Lancaster served as Britain's ultimate strategic asset. Born from the unimpressive and underachieving Avro Manchester twin-engine bomber design, the four-engine Lancaster was tough, rugged, and able to perform effectively at high altitudes. The Lancaster proved to fit the Royal Air Force's (RAF's) need for a heavy, high-altitude, strategic bomber well. From the risky, initial daylight bombing missions over Europe to the fire-bombing of German cities, the Dambuster raid, attacks on Peenemünde and German U-boat bases, and the sinking of the German battleship *Tirpitz*, the Lancaster helped profoundly to secure victory for the Allies in the Second World War. In the post-war era, the Lancaster legend lived on in the form of the Lancastrian transport.

The progressive development of the Lancaster in various marks resulted in numerous performance and specialised mission upgrades to the initial design. One of these specialised marks achieved great fame and glory in the Dambuster raid by destroying vital dams regulating the water supplies for several key heavily populated German towns and cities. Other versions played crucial roles in the destruction of industrial targets, and German cities and battleships.

A total of 7,377 Lancasters were built, one of the highest quantities of heavy bombers produced during the Second World War. The following Lancaster design and development story describes the tremendous combat effectiveness of this important aircraft, which played a vital role in the defeat of Nazi Germany. Throughout the war, the Lancaster's effectiveness as a strategic bomber was demonstrated on countless occasions before the final capitulation of the Axis powers. A total of seventeen Lancasters survive today, with two still flight capable.

The Avro 504O seaplane was an interwar product that was exported to Brazil, Chile, Greece and Japan. A total of seven Avro 504Os were manufactured. The aircraft depicted here is in Greek service. (NARA)

1

AVRO AND ITS PRODUCTS

IN THE BEGINNING

A.V. Roe and Company was founded on 1 January 1910 at Brownsfield Mill, Great Ancoats Street, Manchester, by brothers Alliott and Humphrey Verdon Roe. Humphrey oversaw the company's finances and organisational structure, and also served as managing director, before joining the Royal Flying Corps (RFC) in 1917. Alliott had previously designed the Roe I Triplane, which bore the nickname 'the Bullseye' and was one of the world's first successful aircraft. A.V. Roe built the aircraft in 1909 and in that same year successfully completed the first all-British powered flight. Roy Chadwick rose through the corporate ranks in the company and became chief designer in 1918.

The company's first mass-produced aircraft (a total of eighteen were made), the Avro E or Avro 500, made its maiden flight in March 1912 and were built primarily for the RFC. In the same year, the company manufactured the monoplane Type F, the world's first aeroplane featuring an enclosed crew cabin. A.V. Roe also constructed the biplane Avro Type G in 1912. The Avro 504 was an upgrade from the Type 500 and made its first flight in September 1913. The War Office procured a few of these aircraft prior to the commencement of the First World War. While this aircraft participated in some combat missions at the beginning of the hostilities, it established itself as a primary trainer, a role it continued in until 1933. Over a twenty-year period, 8,340 Avro 504s were produced at several plants, including Hamble, Failsworth, Miles Platting and Newton Heath.

THE INTERWAR PERIOD

Following the First World War, there was a drop in demand for new aircraft orders and Avro experienced a financial crisis in August 1920. Consequently, Crossley Motors obtained 68.5 per cent of Avro's shares and took over its automobile manufacturing business. Avro departed Alexandra Park Aerodrome, in south Manchester, in 1924 for the countryside at New Hall Farm, Woodford, in Cheshire. Crossley Motors sold its Avro shares to Armstrong Siddeley Holdings Ltd in 1928. Also that same year, A.V. Roe left and established the Saunders-Roe company. Avro eventually became a subsidiary of Hawker Siddeley in 1935.

During the 1930s, Avro produced several successful aircraft designs. Among these were the sturdy Avro Tutor biplane trainer and the twin-engine monoplane transport 652. More than 400 Tutors were purchased by the RAF and, with war clouds gathering over Europe, Avro developed the 652 into the Anson coastal reconnaissance aircraft, of which more than 11,000 were built.

The Avro Anson was an interwar product developed during the mid-1930s to serve the RAF as a land-based coastal maritime reconnaissance aircraft. The aircraft proved successful, with 11,020 produced. (NARA)

The Avro 557 Ava was another interwar product that served as a twin-engine. The aircraft was designed during the 1920s for use by the RAF as a torpedo bomber but proved to be unsuccessful, with just two prototypes manufactured. (NARA)

2

DESIGN AND DEVELOPMENT

AN IDEA IS BORN

The idea for the Avro Lancaster was born from the Avro Manchester, a twin-engine medium bomber that possessed unimpressive performance. The Manchester was Avro's submission to British Air Ministry Specification P.13/36 in 1936, which called for the development of a twin-engine medium bomber to be operated 'world-wide', able to carry a torpedo in an internal bomb bay and capable of performing dive bombing. Later additions to the specification called for the incorporation of a mid-mounted cantilever monoplane wing to the design, an all-metal build, and the capability to operate Rolls-Royce Vulture engines for propulsion. Fairey, Boulton Paul, Handley Page and Short all submitted twin-engine candidates.

In February 1937, the Avro 679, also known as the Manchester, was chosen, and a prototype aircraft was requested in April. Manchesters began serving the RAF in November 1940. While the type saw combat during the early part of the Second World War, it proved to be lacking in adequate power and the Vulture engines were often troublesome. In addition, initial versions of the aircraft lacked directional stability, which was remedied by adding an extra central fin. Consequently, a mere 200 Manchesters were produced, with the type being retired in 1942.

The second production Avro Manchester Mk I, L7277, at RAF Boscombe Down in late 1940. (NARA)

A combat operational
Manchester Mk I. (NARA)

A Manchester Mk IA in flight.
(NARA)

A Manchester is prepped for bombing up prior to taking off on a mission during the early part of the Second World War. (NARA)

In 1940, Avro chief design engineer Roy Chadwick commenced the development of an enhanced Manchester. This aircraft was slated to have four Rolls-Royce Merlin engines on wings with increased span; the Merlin engines were less troublesome but also less powerful. The Manchester enhancement was originally dubbed the Type 683 Manchester III but later became known as the Lancaster.

THE LANCASTER PROTOTYPE

The Avro experimental flight department at Ringway Airport, Manchester, built the Lancaster prototype, serial number BT308. The aircraft's base design was a production model Manchester incorporating larger-span wings with four engines. On 9 January 1941, the prototype, with test pilot H.A. 'Sam' Brown at the controls, performed its maiden flight at RAF Ringway, Cheshire. It sported the Manchester I's three-fin tail arrangement but the dorsal tail fin was omitted on the second prototype, DG595. Later production Lancasters made use of a bigger elliptical twin-fin tail arrangement. The modification led to enhanced stability and dorsal gun turret field of fire. In addition, the second prototype featured more powerful Merlin XX engine powerplants.

Frontal view of the Lancaster prototype, serial number BT308. (NARA)

Side view of the prototype.
(NARA)

Rear view of the prototype.
(NARA)

Flight test crews found test-flying the aircraft, which was a marked improvement over the Manchester, enjoyable. Hence the decision was made by British war planners to convert all Manchesters remaining on the assembly line into Lancaster B.Is. Consequently, a corresponding decision was made to outfit twin-engine bomber units with Lancasters. The initial production Lancaster, L7527, flew for the first time in October 1941, powered by Merlin XXs.

Front view of the second production Lancaster, L7528. (NARA)

The second prototype Lancaster, DG595, in flight on 22 August 1941. (WW2images)

Frontal view of the second production Lancaster, L7528. (NARA)

Side view of L7528. (NARA)

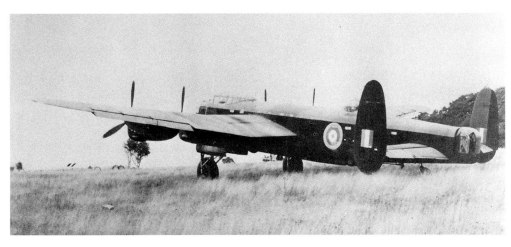

Rear view of L7528. (NARA)

LANCASTER I TACTICAL FLIGHT TRIALS

On 24 April 1942, a series of important tactical flight trials of a production variant Lancaster I were conducted by the Air Fighting Development Unit (AFDU) at RAF Duxford. The trials aimed to determine how the heavy bomber could best be used in combat and were performed by a crew from 44 Squadron. As stated in the official British Tactical Trials Report No. 47, 'A tactical circus of 3 Spitfires then visited all the Lancaster Squadrons in 5 Group, Bomber Command, and carried out a series of affiliations both with single aircraft and with various formations.'[1]

The approximate weight of the test aircraft was 60,200lb, with a maximum bomb load of 12,000lb. Exceptions to this were made for special missions, in which the aircraft was made capable of transporting 14,000lb. On missions in which the aircraft carried a 12,000lb load, the aircraft possessed a range of 1,100 to 1,200 miles. The Lancaster had a maximum range of 2,000 miles with only a 4,000lb bomb load.

During the tactical flight trials, the aircraft had a seven-man aircrew, which included a captain and second pilot, who piloted the aeroplane; an air observer, who served as navigator and bomb aimer; a first air gunner, who acted as a wireless communications operator/gunner; a second wireless operator/air gunner, who operated the front turret; an air gunner, who operated the mid-upper turret; and another air gunner in the tail turret.

According to the official British Lancaster I tactical flight trials report:

The Lancaster is reasonably manoeuvrable for a large aircraft. The controls are positive and moderately heavy under normal cruising conditions, but tend to stiffen appreciably as speed is increased over 200 m.p.h. Where any evasive manoeuvres are attempted, however, there is a considerable lag in the aileron control and this is very marked when the aircraft is fully loaded. This means that considerable practice is required before violent evasion is possible at ground level. The cruising speed is approximately 185 m.p.h., I.A.S., when light. The maximum speed near the ground at a weight of 60,000 lbs., is approximately 220 m.p.h., I.A.S.[2]

The main objective of the flight trials was to determine the optimum evasion method to be performed by the Lancaster against simulated attacks by single fighters or a group of fighters at the same time. As concluded by the Wing Commander, Commanding, AFDU on 30 May 1942:

General

The Lancaster is capable of carrying a large bomb load at a good cruising speed. Its range is superior to that of other heavy bombers except the Liberator. Aileron control when fully loaded is not good, but the aircraft is still very manoeuvrable for its size.

Armament

The armament of the Lancaster at present consisting of nose, mid-upper and tail turrets, is good. The field of fire of the upper turret towards the rear is only moderately satisfactory.

The new under-turret – the F.N. 64 – which is not yet in the service, is of considerable value for daylight operations.

Adequate armour protection against 7.9mm machine guns is provided for the crew.

Tactical

The field of view of the crew is satisfactory and good fighting control can be carried out.

For a single aircraft the best evasion against astern, quarter or beam attacks is the corkscrew or the tight turn.

Against head-on attacks a turn and dive is effective.

For formation flying a vic of three is the most suitable unit. For high or low level attacks the best evasion is by individual action by each of the 3 aircraft. The leader should undulate steeply while Nos. 2 & 3 corkscrew on either side of him. This can be done without losing the value of mutual fire support. It enables the formation to maintain track towards their target while giving attacking fighters difficult deflection shooting.

If intercepted during a low-level operation, it is essential for a formation to climb up to about 600 feet to give themselves room for evasive action. Evasion by low flying only is not effective.[3]

The Lancaster's defensive armament originally consisted of four Nash & Thompson Frazer-Nash hydraulically controlled turrets positioned in the aircraft's nose, tail and mid-upper- and underside. At first, the tail turret featured four Browning .303 Mark II machine guns, while the other turrets were armed with two similar machine guns.

The Lancaster B.I used in the Production Variant Tactical Flight Trials conducted by the Air Fighting Development Unit at Duxford on 24 April 1942. Note the ventral gun turret on the aircraft. (NARA)

The first contract requested by Bomber Command from Avro consisted of 1,070 bombers.[4] Most Lancasters were built at Avro's Chadderton factory, located near Oldham, Lancashire. The aircraft were flight-tested at Woodford Aerodrome in Cheshire. When the demand for Lancasters surpassed Avro's manufacturing capability, the decision was made to establish the Lancaster Aircraft Group, which consisted of several companies that agreed to undertake complete or component construction.

Metropolitan-Vickers and Armstrong Whitworth also built Lancasters. In addition, Austin Motor Company Works in Longbridge, Birmingham, built them during the latter portion of the war, while Vickers-Armstrongs at Chester and Castle Bromwich, Birmingham, built Lancasters post-war.

In addition to being built in the United Kingdom, the Lancaster was also manufactured by Victory Aircraft in Malton, Ontario, Canada, beginning in 1942. The late-war, Canadian-built Lancaster B.X was the only Canadian-manufactured variant to be built in notable quantity (430). A total of 7,377 Lancasters were constructed.

Lancaster B.Is were produced until February 1946, with some of the first featuring a ventral gun turret. This was later omitted as Bomber Command shifted priorities from daylight Lancaster missions to night-time operations.

Frontal view of Lancaster B.I R5727, which became the first of its type to fly across the Atlantic. This aircraft served as the example aircraft from which Canadian-made Lancasters were produced. The aircraft is shown at Prestwick Airport prior to making the historic flight to Canada in August 1942. (NARA)

Lancaster B.I R5727 in flight on 16 September 1942. Note the ventral gun turret on the fuselage underside aft of the bomb bay. (NARA)

Lancaster B.I R5727 climbs on 16 September 1942. (NARA)

Lancaster B.I R5727 in flight. The ventral gun turret is clearly visible. (NARA)

Top view of Lancaster B.I R5727. Note the camouflage scheme on the upper surfaces. (NARA)

Lancaster B.I R5727 taxies in after performing a flight. (NARA)

A Lancaster B.I in flight. Note the Rolls-Royce Merlin engines. (NARA)

A view from underneath the same aircraft as top right. (NARA)

A top view of the same aircraft.
(NARA)

A Lancaster B.I on a bombing mission. (NARA)

OTHER LANCASTER VARIANTS

The Lancaster B.III featured Packard Merlins and a total of 3,030 were produced, primarily at Avro's Newton Heath factory.

A total of thirty-two Lancaster B.I Specials were developed to carry the Tallboy and Grand Slam mega-bombs. These aircraft featured enhanced engines that were equipped with paddle-bladed propellers for better propulsion. The aircraft also had their gun turrets removed for weight reduction and improved aerodynamic performance. To accommodate the Tallboy, the bomb bay doors were modified to feature a distinct bulge in shape; these were removed entirely and the bomb bay faired over to facilitate the Grand Slam.

The PR.I was a specially modified B.I developed for photographic reconnaissance with a camera nestled in the bomb bay. PR.Is flew with the RAF's 82 and 541 Squadrons during the war. They were devoid of any armament and their noses were reconfigured.

Front view of a Lancaster B.III at Wright Field in Dayton, Ohio, on 21 July 1943. (NARA)

Side view of the same aircraft. Note the engine exhaust flame dampeners have been removed from the engines. (NARA)

Rear view of the same aircraft. (NARA)

The B.I (FE), a tropical version of the late-war Lancaster, was slated for use in the Pacific.

The B.II featured Bristol Hercules (Hercules VI or XVI) engines built to mitigate the shortage of Merlin engines so desperately needed for British fighter aircraft. Three hundred were built by Armstrong Whitworth. When Luftwaffe night fighters began employing *Schräge Musik* tactics, which saw them carry upward-facing armament, provisions were made for the B.II to carry a 20mm (0.79in) cannon or a 50in (13mm) machine gun in the opening left by the deletion of the FN.64 ventral turret to counter the threat. Later, some aircraft had a .303in (7.7mm) machine gun in this position. In later Lancaster variants, the H2S radar was positioned here.

The Lancaster B.III (Special) became known as the 'Type 464 Provisioning' or 'Dambuster', of which twenty-three were produced. These were modified to carry the Upkeep bouncing bomb used in dam-busting missions. In these aircraft the bomb bay doors were omitted and replaced with special Vickers-made struts to carry the bomb, which was spun by a specially fitted hydraulic motor. In addition, the mid-upper turret was deleted as a weight-saving measure.

The Lancaster ASR.III/ASR.3 was essentially a B.III specially designed for air-sea rescue missions. The ASR.III/ASR.3 was equipped with three dipole ventral antennae aft of the radome. In addition, the aircraft carried an airborne lifeboat in a specially modified bomb bay. This variant was devoid of armament and had a fairing where the mid-upper turret used to be.

Front view of the Lancaster B.II prototype. (NARA)

Front view of the Lancaster B.II prototype. (NARA)

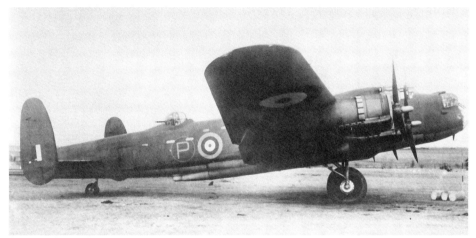

Side view of the Lancaster B.II prototype. (NARA)

Rear view of the Lancaster B.II prototype. (NARA)

A Hercules-powered Lancaster B.II DS771 in flight prior to delivery to 426 Squadron. (WW2images)

The GR.3/MR.3 was a modified B.III designed for maritime reconnaissance.

The Lancaster IV had a lengthened wing span and fuselage as well as an updated Boulton Paul F turret that featured two 0.5in Browning machine guns. The variant also possessed a framed 'bay window' nose glazing. The type later became known as the Lincoln I.

The Lancaster V featured a larger wingspan and longer fuselage, and was powered by two-stage Merlin 85 engines. It later became the Lincoln II.

The B.VI was a further development of the B.III, of which only nine were built. These featured Merlin 85/87 two-stage supercharged engines that provided enhanced high-altitude capability. The B.VI was capable of a maximum speed of 313mph at 18,200ft and could reach a maximum altitude of 28,500ft. The aircraft also had three-bladed, paddle-type propellers. B.VIs served pathfinder squadrons only: 7, 83 and 635 Squadrons, RAF; and 405 Squadron, Royal Canadian Air Force (RCAF).

The B.VII was the last production variant.

The B.X was produced by Canada and featured Canadian/US-manufactured instruments and electronics. In subsequent production B.Xs, the Martin 250 CE replaced the Nash & Thompson FN-50 mid-upper turret. The B.XV was also produced in Canada and later redesignated as the Lincoln XV. Only one example was manufactured.

An Avro Lincoln II, featuring Packard Merlin engines, in March 1945. (NARA)

The Canadian Lancaster B.XV/Lincoln XV.
(Canadian forces)

BOMBSIGHT TECHNOLOGIES USED BY LANCASTERS

The Lancaster's bombsight technology gradually improved over the course of the aircraft's development. During the early years of the Second World War, Lancasters used the Mark IX Course Setting Bomb Sight (CSBS), a preset vector unit, the use of which entailed squinting through wires set manually to the aeroplane's velocity, altitude and bombload. The bombsight proved to be primitive and limited in terms of operational flexibility.

The Mark XIV was a more advanced version: a vector bombsight in which the bomb aimer inputted data concerning the bombload, target altitude and wind direction into an analogue computer. This then calculated bomb trajectory and presented an inverted sword shape on a sight glass positioned on a sighting head. Once the target appeared in the crosshairs of the sword shape, the bomb aimer released the bombs, usually with great accuracy.

Some Lancasters were equipped with T1 bombsights, which were essentially modified Mark XIVs slated for mass production, manufactured in the United States.

No. 617 Squadron Lancasters made use of the Stabilising Automatic Bomb Sight (SABS), an advanced model specifically designed for precision. The SABS was a tachometric sight, similar to the US Norden type.

3

FIRST COMBAT MISSIONS

DAYLIGHT OPERATIONS

No. 44 Squadron served as the initial Lancaster conversion squadron in early 1942. This squadron called RAF Waddington in Lincolnshire home. No. 97 Squadron, also stationed at Waddington, soon followed suit. The first combat operational mission was on 2 March 1942 and involved the deployment of naval mines in the Heligoland Bight. The mission was carried out by 44 Squadron Lancasters. They also bombed the German city of Essen, North Rhine-Westphalia, on 10 March.

On 24 March 1942 the Lancaster suffered its first loss, when R5493 was shot down by German anti-aircraft guns over Lorient, France. As a result of mounting Lancaster losses experienced during daytime missions, Bomber Command decided to use the type primarily at night. However, success was achieved by twelve Lancasters belonging to 44 and 99 Squadrons that bombed the Maschinenfabrik Augsburg-Nürnberg AG engine manufacturing plant in southern Germany on 17 April 1942 during the daytime. This despite losing three of their own to German Bf 109 fighters over France, as well as two additional bombers as a result of enemy anti-aircraft fire from the plant. Nos 44 and 99 Squadron Lancasters were less successful on 27 April, when they failed to damage the German battleship *Tirpitz* in a small-scale, daylight mission.

No. 97 Squadron Lancasters perform a low-level practice mission on 16 April 1942 in a prelude to the Augsburg bombing mission. (Royal Air Force official photographer)

In June 1942, five 44 Squadron Lancasters were assigned to Nutts Corner in County Antrim, Northern Ireland, for anti-U-boat duty. The unit conducted two raids against enemy submarines throughout its short stay and registered one kill, by Flight Lieutenant T.P.C. Barlow, DFC. In addition, 61 Squadron assigned eight Lancasters to RAF St Eval in Cornwall on 16 July for a five-week stay in which they managed to sink one U-boat on their initial mission.

4

BOMBING GERMAN CITIES

NIGHT MISSIONS

The Thousand-Bomber Raids

The decision made by the British to bomb German cities was largely made on a logical and political basis. The main objective of conducting such an air campaign was to crush the will of the German people to continue fighting the war. Britain's ally Russia was in a dire situation fighting the Germans in the east, and British Prime Minister Winston Churchill wanted to show his allies (the United States of America as well) that the British were capable of striking the heart of the enemy, its civil population. RAF Bomber Command served as the only means by which Britain could accomplish this feat.

As stated in *Lancaster: The Backbone of Bomber Command*:

The War Cabinet and the Air Ministry therefore drew up a plan for a revolutionary new offensive, under which 43 leading German industrial cities, with a combined population of 15 million, would come under continuous attack. These attacks would be made against the cities themselves, and not just against factories within them; Churchill himself approved the switch from attempts at precision bombing to what was a deliberate area bombing strategy.[1]

Bomber Command Air Officer Commanding-in-Chief (AOC-in-C) Air Chief Marshal Sir Arthur Harris, a big advocate of fire-bombing German cities, soon proclaimed:

The Nazis entered this war under the rather childish delusion that they were going to bomb everyone else, and nobody was going to bomb them. At Rotterdam, London, Warsaw and half a hundred other places, they put their rather naive theory into operation. They sowed the wind, and now they are going to reap the whirlwind.[2]

Harris's primary strategy for the bombing offensive was to conduct concentrated missions in short time periods so as to exhaust enemy defensive and emergency forces.

The first massive Lancaster night mission occurred on the night of 30 May 1942, when Lancasters took part in Operation Millennium – the initial Thousand-Bomber Raid carried out against the German city of Köln. Out of the thousand RAF bombers participating in the raid, only 400 came from front-line Bomber Command squadrons. The remaining aircraft and crews were called up from operational training squadrons. For instance, 49 out of a force of 208 aircraft from 91 Group were piloted by students. A total of 1,047 bombers ultimately took part in the mission and wreaked tremendous devastation on the beautiful cathedral city located on the Rhine River.

Approximately seventy-three Lancasters participated in the mission, with all of the aircraft coming from 5 Group. This force included fifteen aircraft from 83 Squadron, eleven from 106 Squadron and one from 50 Squadron. These Lancasters were joined by 131 Halifaxes from 4 Group, 88 Stirlings from 3 Group and 602 Wellingtons.

A total of 868 aircraft bombed the main target and dropped 1,455 tons of bombs. Most of the bombs were incendiaries, which engulfed the target in flames within ninety minutes. A total of 3,330 buildings were destroyed, with many other buildings suffering some form of damage. An estimated 486 German lives were lost in the attack, with 45,132 made homeless. Approximately 150,000 Germans escaped the city. A total of forty-one bombers were lost during the mission, with only one of these a Lancaster.

A Lancaster B.III in flight.
(Royal Air Force)

No. 83 Squadron Lancaster B.I R5852 'OL-Y'. This aircraft was based at Scampton, Lincolnshire. (WW2images)

No. 83 Squadron Lancaster B.I R5620 'OL-H' prepares to lead the remaining squadron Lancasters on take-off from their base at Scampton in June 1942. The bombers were heading out to participate in the Thousand-Bomber Raid on Bremen. (WW2images)

The bomber force assembled for the Köln mission was used once again on the night of 1–2 June 1942 for an attack on the German city of Essen. This force consisted of 956 aircraft, of which seventy-four were Lancasters. The results of this mission, however, were far less successful, with damage insignificant as a result of haze obscuring the target area. A total of thirty-one bombers were lost, with four being Lancasters.

The last and biggest Thousand-Bomber Raid was mounted on Bremen by an attacking force of 960 bombers on the night of 4–5 June 1942. Approximately 10 per cent of this force were Lancasters (sixteen aircraft each from 83, 97 and 207 Squadrons; seventeen from 106; fourteen from 61; and twelve from 44). A total of 1,067 aircraft participated in this raid, which lasted sixty-five minutes. Weather conditions were conducive to generating a firestorm that resulted in the decimation of 572 houses and the deaths of eighty-five civilians. No. 5 Group was ordered to bomb the Focke-Wulf factory, which was heavily damaged, while Coastal Command aircraft despatched for the raid managed to damage the Deschimag shipyard. A total of forty-four aircraft were lost over the target, with four more shot down over the North Sea while returning to their home bases. These losses were Bomber Command's greatest thus far in the war.

No. 83 Squadron Lancaster B.I R5626 'OL-M' lands at Scampton in 1942. The aircraft on the ground in the background is a Manchester. (WW2images)

Other Notable German City Bombing Missions

On the night of 31 July–1 August, a force of 100-plus Lancasters contributed to the fire-bombing of the German city of Düsseldorf.

In November 1942, Lancasters bombed Osnabrück, while in December they targeted Duisburg. A strike force entirely comprising Lancasters bombed Berlin on 16 January 1943. The attack caused insignificant damage to the German capital, but did have a psychological effect on the city's populace. Seventy-nine Lancasters bombed Berlin again on 1 March.

Bomber Command commenced the Battle of the Ruhr on 5 March 1943 by launching a massive raid on Essen. The strike force was made up of 412 bombers (140 Lancasters). Lancasters bombed Stuttgart on 15 April and Plzeň the next day. Throughout the remainder of April, Lancasters bombed Stettin, Duisburg and the Ruhr. The Ruhr remained the primary target of Bomber Command during the month of May.

Operation Gomorrah – heavy, round-the-clock fire-bombing of the city of Hamburg – commenced in late July 1943 and lasted through early August 1943. The most destructive of these attacks occurred on the night of 27 July, when a force of 787 RAF bombers that included 74 Vickers Wellingtons, 116 Short Stirlings, 244 Handley Page Halifaxes and 353 Lancasters laid waste to the city. Tremendous firestorms caused the death of some 18,474 Germans. A total of 8,621 tons of bombs were expended during the operation.

Lancasters took part in the bombing of Hanover in September 1943 and raids on several German cities in October, including Munich, Kassel, Frankfurt, Offenbach, Ludwigshafen, Stuttgart, Friedrichshafen and Leipzig.

Under the direction of Churchill and Air Chief Marshal Harris, Lancasters took part in the relentless bombing of Berlin from 15 November 1943 to 24 November 1944. During this period, no fewer than sixteen major bombing operations targeted Berlin. A total of 9,111 missions were undertaken by Allied bombers, with 7,256 flown by Lancasters.

A formation of No. 619 Squadron Lancaster B.IIIs in flight. The aircraft were based at Coningsby, Lincolnshire. (WW2images)

A 170 Squadron Lancaster in flight. This particular aircraft has a gas-detection dish on the nose and features a Rose rear turret. (WW2images)

A 15 Squadron Lancaster in flight. The two yellow fin bars indicate that the aircraft is GEE-H leader. (WW2images)

Ground crews prepare to load 4,000lb Mark I HC bombs ('cookies') on an 83 Squadron Lancaster B.I at Mildenhall, Suffolk. (WW2images)

Clockwise from left: A 1 Group Lancaster flies over Hamburg during a night raid on the city on 30–31 January 1943. The aircraft is silhouetted against flares, smoke and explosions. (WW2images); A Lancaster returns to its base following a successful raid on Berlin on the night of 2–3 January 1944. (NARA); A snowy scene at a RAF Bomber Command airfield in February 1944 in which a 4,000lb HC 'cookie' bomb is being loaded in the bomb bay of a waiting Lancaster. The heavy bombers were being prepped for a raid on German industrial centres. (NARA)

A RAF Lancaster B.III takes to the sky at dusk on a bombing mission over Germany in 1944. (NARA)

A 463 Squadron Royal Australian Air Force (RAAF) Lancaster undergoes overhaul in a hangar at Waddington in August 1944. (Australian War Memorial)

A 463 Squadron RAAF Lancaster takes off from Waddington on a bombing mission in August 1944. (Royal Australian Air Force)

A Lancaster awaits the signal to take off at night. (WW2images)

No. 467 Squadron RAAF Lancaster 'S for Sugar' is prepped for its ninety-seventh combat mission at Waddington in 1944. (Press Agency photographer, via Australian War Memorial)

A Lancaster B.II in flight. (Unknown photographer)

A Castle Bromwich-stationed Lancaster, possibly being piloted by Alex Henshaw, performs a test flight. (WW2images)

Air and ground crew of 467 Squadron RAAF Lancaster 'S for Sugar' celebrate the aircraft's successful completion of 100 missions in May 1944. (WW2images)

No. 49 Squadron Lancaster B.III DV238 'EA-O' is tractored to the dispersal site at Fiskerton, Lincolnshire, by Leading Aircraftwoman Lilian Yule. (WW2images)

RAAF Lancaster 'G for George' in 1945. (Australian War Memorial)

One of the most devastating and morally controversial night raids on a German city was that on Dresden on the night of 13–14 February 1945. Bomber Command launched other diversionary attacks to confound German air defence forces, with 360 Lancasters and Halifaxes raiding a synthetic oil plant in Böhlen and 71 de Havilland Mosquitos striking Magdeburg. A formation of Lancasters from 83 Squadron, 5 Group, and Mosquitos performed pathfinding duties, dropping magnesium parachute flares so as to mark the target area for the primary force, which consisted of 796 Lancasters. These bombers carried 500 tons of high explosives and 375 tons of incendiaries.

In a second raid on the city several hours later, Lancasters from 1, 3, 6 and 8 Groups further fire-bombed the target. A total of 1,800 tons of bombs were dropped by Lancasters during the second raid, which killed in excess of 50,000 people. The city was also bombed by the United States Army Air Forces (USAAF) during the daylight hours of 14–15 February, suffering 25,000 casualties, with most victims perishing in the tremendous firestorms generated by incendiaries.

A RAF Bomber Command station ground crew returns the V-sign to a nearby searchlight crew with the nose of a Lancaster silhouetted in 1945. (NARA)

5

TARGETING PEENEMÜNDE

On the night of 17–18 August 1943, Bomber Command launched perhaps one of the most significant missions of the Second World War: the bombing of the German rocket research operation at Peenemünde on the Baltic coast. Approximately 324 Lancasters, 218 Halifaxes and 54 Stirlings took part in the raid. Pathfinder aircraft marked the target area, which included the scientists' accommodation, the rocket manufacturing facility and experimental facilities. The bombers wreaked much devastation, killing 180 senior personnel in the process, and delaying the development of the V-2 rocket for several months. Unfortunately for Bomber Command, forty bombers, including twenty-three Lancasters, were lost.

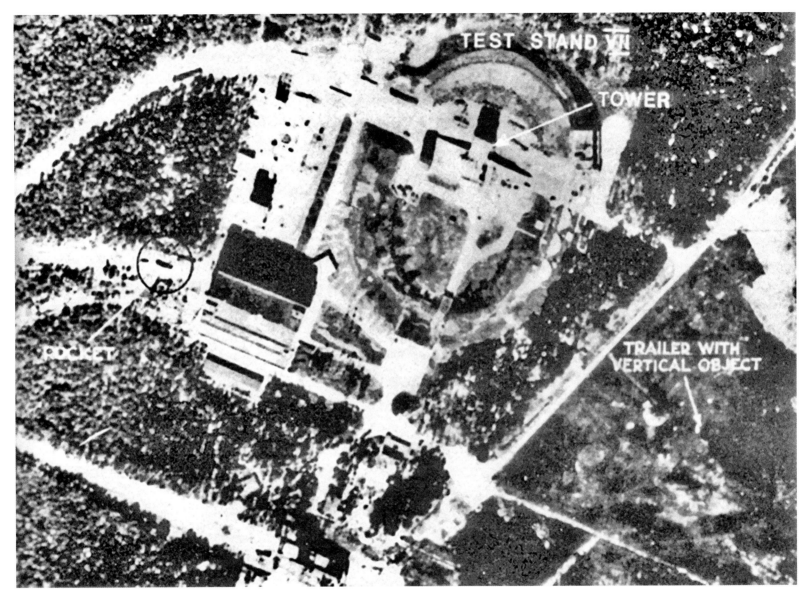

A RAF reconnaissance photo depicting V-2 rockets at Peenemünde Test Stands I and VII on 12 June 1943. (RAF)

6

U-BOAT BASES

At the beginning of 1943, planners within the War Cabinet ordered Bomber Command to launch area raids on several French port cities, including operational U-boat bases. The raids targeted Lorient, St-Nazaire, Brest and La Pallice. These raids not only served strategic purposes, but also acted as diversions from the bombing offensive against German cities. Bomber Command raids against the U-boat bases were designed to wreak devastation on maintenance facilities; power, water, and light services; and local U-boat servicing workers. While the raids caused little damage to the submarines and servicing facilities, tremendous damage was inflicted on the French cities and general populace.

Bomber Command's task of causing significant damage to the U-boat bases was made more challenging due to the fact that the Germans reinforced the U-boat pens with thick concrete. The raids on Lorient and St-Nazaire were particularly heavy. On the night of 7–8 February, an attacking force of 323 bombers, including 80 Lancasters, pummelled Lorient, causing widespread devastation. A total of three Lancasters were lost during the raid. A single raid on Lorient on the night of 13–14 February, in which 164 Lancasters took part, marked the first time that Bomber Command dropped in excess of 1,000 tons of bombs. Insignificant bombing results on these first missions caused Bomber Command to abandon raids against Brest and La Pallice.

7

THE DAM-BUSTING MISSIONS OF OPERATION CHASTISE

The Lancaster is perhaps best known for its remarkable performance in the dam-busting missions of Operation Chastise. At the beginning of summer 1943, this operation, to destroy German dams, commenced at the direction of Air Chief Marshal Harris. Nineteen modified Provisioning Lancaster B.Is of 617 Squadron dropped Upkeep mines or 'bouncing bombs' in an attack on the Möhne, Eder and Sorpe dams on the evening of 16–17 May. The bombers attacked in three waves. The initial wave, which consisted of nine aircraft, suffered one casualty to flak while flying to the target. The specially modified Lancasters dropped five Upkeeps against the Möhne dam with the loss of only one aircraft. There were only three Upkeeps left, which were expended in another successful attack on the Eder dam. An additional pair of Lancasters were shot down on the way back to their home base.

The second dam-busting Lancaster wave experienced more difficulty in attacking their target, the Sorpe dam. This proved to be more difficult to breach due to its different construction – a core made of concrete that was reinforced by concrete-capped earth banks. The Lancasters encountered heavy defences that had already been alerted by the first wave, and two aircraft were shot down and an additional two had to turn back towards home. The last remaining Lancaster performed a brave attack on the dam but its results were deemed inconclusive.

THE DAMBUSTERS SQUADRON

No. 617 Squadron, which operated Lancasters, was secretly established at RAF Scampton on 21 March 1943. It comprised Royal Canadian Air Force, Royal Australian Air Force and Royal New Zealand Air Force personnel. The squadron's primary mission was to breach the three primary dams that supplied water and power to the Ruhr in Germany, using the Upkeep mine that had been brilliantly conceived by engineer and inventor Barnes Wallis. These three dams were the Möhne, Eder, and Sorpe. The mission was dubbed Operation Chastise and carried out on 17 May 1943. The squadron was commanded by Wing Commander Guy Gibson.

Following the completion of the dam-busting raids, Gibson received the Victoria Cross for the vital leadership he provided during the mission and Gibson was then relieved of his flying duties to embark on a publicity tour. He later returned to Bomber Command service. Gibson completed in excess of 170 combat missions before perishing when his 627 Squadron Mosquito was damaged during bombing missions against Rheydt and Mönchengladbach on the night of 19 September 1944 and crashed at Steenbergen, The Netherlands, before bursting into flames. Gibson was only 26 years old at the time of his death. No. 617 Squadron went on to take part in the destruction of the German battleship *Tirpitz*, using Tallboy bombs. The squadron also carried out several precision-bombing missions, dropping Tallboy and Grand Slam bombs on concrete U-boat bunkers and bridges.

The third dam-busting Lancaster wave was launched at midnight and was intended to serve as a reserve force. It was met with heavy opposition. On the way to the target, two Lancasters were lost. Nevertheless, Flight Sergeant Brown pressed home the attack on the Sorpe dam while Flight Sergeant Townsend attacked a target that was mistakenly assumed to be the Enepe dam. However, he was later ordered to perform a final visual reconnaissance of the Möhne dam. All of this was done at 270mph, the aircraft's top speed, and at a low altitude. Townsend eventually completed the harrowing journey back to his home base, being forced to shut down one engine in the process. The last Lancaster of the third wave had to turn back due to its turret being knocked out of commission and navigational problems resulting from fog build-up.

A total of 330 million tons of water were dispersed by the pair of breached dams. Approximately 1,294 Germans drowned in the areas downstream of the Möhne dam, with nearly half the casualties being Russian and Ukrainian prisoners of war (PoWs). The waters released by the breached dams caused the destruction of three power stations and five pumping plants, with an additional twelve pumping plants sustaining significant damage. The successful missions caused the loss of much livestock. The Ruhr's water supplies were also adversely affected for one month. In addition, the raids resulted in the disruption of domestic electricity to Bochum, Dortmund, Hagen and Hamm.

While damage caused by the Eder dam breaching was more significant, there was less loss of human life. A total of twenty-five road and rail bridges were destroyed. The train station in Giflitz and the bridge and main line to Hamburg were also destroyed. As a result of the breaching of the Eder dam, the Fulda and Weser rivers required dredging. Bridges and banks also had to be repaired.

As a result of the successful missions, an extraordinary amount of personnel had to be diverted from other critical services to participate in the repair effort, and this inhibited the completion of Normandy defences prior to D-Day. A total of eight Lancasters of the nineteen that participated in Operation Chastise missions were lost.

In this photo showing a 617 Squadron Upkeep mine practice dropping sequence taken at Reculver bombing range, Flight Lieutenant J.L. Munro, piloting Provisioning Lancaster ED921/G, flies on after successfully releasing his bomb. This struck the water, causing a plume of spray to rise up in the air and consume the Lancaster's tail, which resulted in damage to the bomber and an extremely wet rear gunner. Meanwhile, the bomb bounced off the water and struck the target. (IWM staff photographers)

A RAF reconnaissance photo taken on 17 May 1943 of the breached Möhne dam. (Flying Officer Jerry Fray RAF)

8

OPERATION CROSSBOW

Lancasters played a crucial strategic role in Operation Crossbow, the destruction of V (Vengeance) weapon sites throughout Europe, with No. 617 Squadron designated to take part. In the winter of 1943–44, 617 Squadron commenced raids on V-1 flying bomb launch sites. These sites were heavily concentrated in the Pas-de-Calais area of Nazi-occupied France. The task proved to be challenging due to the fact that the sites were small and well camouflaged. The Lancasters, now equipped with a new bombsight, were assisted by Oboe radar-equipped Mosquitos of the Pathfinder Force (8 Group). The Mosquitos were at the tip of the spear of the attacking force, marking targets. The first attacks proved to be ineffective; however, better results were later achieved and some of the sites were put out of commission. Nevertheless, the Germans set up a multitude of launch locations that 617 Squadron could not take out alone.

Leonard Cheshire, one of the RAF's most famous bomber pilots, made the decision to have 617 Squadron mark its own targets. He soon devised tactics for attacking the V-1 launch sites whereby he (in his Lancaster) would fly into the target at a low altitude, leading the squadron's remaining aircraft. Following identification of the target, a task made difficult by the presence of heavy and precise flak, he would drop flares or coloured markers prior to ordering the remaining Lancasters at a higher altitude to engage. Cheshire was then to circle the target, directing and monitoring the results of the raid.

After learning that the Germans could launch V-1s from swiftly constructed prefabricated ramps, the Allies sought to eliminate the V-1s while they were being stored in underground concrete shelters. Bomber Command decided to use Tallboy special deep-penetration bombs to take out the shelters and 617 Squadron was assigned these important missions. The squadron undertook attacks against sites at Mimoyecques, Nucourt, Watten and Wizernes.

On 19 June 1944, 617 Lancasters attacked Watten, with nineteen bombers dropping fifteen Tallboys on the target. The V-1 storage site at Wizernes was demolished after five direct Tallboy hits on 24 June. Only one Lancaster was lost on this mission.

A 514 Squadron Lancaster, stationed at Waterbeach, Cambridgeshire, drops its bombs on a flying-bomb launch site at Les Catelliers, France, during Operation Crossbow. (WW2images)

9

TACTICAL MISSIONS IN SUPPORT OF D-DAY

Air Chief Marshal Harris decided to use Bomber Command to support the Allied invasion of Normandy on D-Day and on 14 April 1944 its aircraft began attacking pre-invasion targets. Lancaster squadrons bombed railway targets in western Germany, Belgium and France in missions that gradually increased in intensity as the Allies tried to cut off reinforcements supplied to German forces in Normandy via rail. Other high-priority targets such as military camps, armament dumps, depots and factories were also targeted. In addition, an effort was made to cut off reinforcements and supplies to the Pas-de-Calais area in a deceptive move to make the Germans think that the actual invasion would occur there.

During the course of the tactical D-Day support missions, bombing techniques and targeting accuracy improved significantly. For example, Mosquitos were used more for target marking by 8 and 5 Groups. No. 5 Group quickly initiated operations as its own force after it regained 97 and 83 Squadrons from pathfinding duties. No. 5 Group also formed its own Mosquito squadron, 627 Squadron. No. 617 formed a large Mosquito force used exclusively as target-marking aircraft.

Legendary Commanding Officer Wing Commander Leonard Cheshire of 617 Squadron perfected the target-marking technique during a raid on a German aircraft factory in Toulouse on 5–6 April. Cheshire used the swift Mosquito to his advantage, performing three flyovers of the target at low altitude prior to dropping his markers. These were then supplemented by markers released from two 617 Squadron Lancasters. Regular 5 Group Lancaster squadrons then proceeded to bomb the target with outstanding results. As a result, the target-marking technique was officially adopted and led to a drastic improvement in bombing accuracy. Other Lancaster units were experiencing an average bombing error of 680 yards; in comparison, following adoption of the technique, 5 Group experienced an average bombing error of 380 yards.

When Bomber Command commenced its missions in support of D-Day against targets in France, the Lancaster served as the primary heavy bomber. At this time Bomber Command had forty squadrons flying Lancasters, the majority B.Is and B.IIIs, with some B.IIs also included. No. 408 Squadron's B.IIs were responsible for the destruction of coastal gun emplacements at Longues on the first morning of D-Day. The remaining pair of B.II squadrons experienced only light casualty rates, which permitted their use into autumn 1944. No. 514 Squadron's B.IIs were replaced by B.Is and B.IIIs from June to the end of September, while 408 Squadron's were replaced by Halifax B.IIIs in August 1944.

The raids on coastal gun positions commenced in early May. During the week prior to the invasion, Lancasters bombed German radio listening stations, radar installations and radar-jamming facilities. In addition, the bombers dropped arms and equipment to resistance personnel.

Bomber Command set a record by flying 1,211 D-Day support missions on the eve of the invasion. Many of these entailed bombing enemy troop positions, gun positions, ammunition and oil dumps, and road and rail communications. Lancasters also took part in raids on German E-boats and light offensive vessels in French ports.

At times, Lancasters performed close air support missions, during which they attacked German positions located close to Allied ground forces.

Following the invasion, Bomber Command continued to raid German oil targets, particularly in the Ruhr. Lancaster day bombing resumed because Allied escort fighters could now escort the heavies for the duration of their missions, thereby significantly reducing casualties.

On 15 August, a force of 1,004 bombers (of which 599 were Lancasters) raided nine night-fighter airfields. These attacks were conducted just before the resumption of the night-bombing missions against German cities. The tactical D-Day support bombing missions and attacks on the German night-fighter airfields helped signal the demise of the *Jagdwaffe* and *Nachtjagdwaffe*.

The tactical D-Day support bombing missions proved Bomber Command's effectiveness in carrying out pinpoint-bombing missions with a high level of accuracy.

RAAF Lancasters daylight bomb German troop positions near Caen, France, on 18 June 1944. (Australian War Memorial)

10

SINKING GERMAN WARSHIPS

During the latter years of the Second World War, the Lancaster proved to be quite effective in undertaking devastating attacks against German warships. By mid-1942, Bomber Command had failed to achieve any successes in bombing missions against enemy warships. The command was unable to halt the escapes of the battleships *Scharnhorst* and *Gneisenau* or the battlecruiser *Prinz Eugen* during the 'Channel Dash' of 12 February 1942. Moreover, after several attacks, Bomber Command was unable to significantly damage the battleship *Tirpitz* while it was moored in its Norwegian lair. A major inhibiting issue proved to be Bomber Command's lack of the right type of weapon to successfully perform this mission. However, several establishments were hard at work devising potential solutions.

One of these that showed substantial potential was the Capital Ship Bomb. This weapon weighed 5,600lb and featured a hollow-charge warhead. Many people likened it to an 'elongated turnip'. The bomb was designed to penetrate an armoured deck prior to exploding and obliterating the ship's bottom. At the time, the Royal Navy considered the aircraft carrier *Graf Zeppelin* to be the German warship that posed the greatest threat to the Allies. The final construction of the carrier, in the Polish port of Gdynia, was almost complete. In addition, the warships that had succeeded in making the Channel Dash were also moored there.

A total of four Capital Ship Bombs had been built by the time Gdynia had been made a high-priority target by Bomber Command. Wing Commander Guy Gibson's 106 Squadron was chosen by Bomber Command to perform the mission. Six aircrews began training for this special sortie, while six Lancasters were modified to accommodate the Capital Ship Bomb. Production of the ordnance proved to be expensive and complex, and ballistic trials indicated that it possessed a highly irregular and unpredictable trajectory. This would greatly reduce bombing accuracy, unless performed at an extremely low altitude.

However, rather than dropping the Capital Ship Bombs from an altitude of 1,000ft, which would expose the Lancasters to more intense flak, the decision was made to carry out the mission at 6,000ft. This did not bode well for its success. Three 106 Squadron Lancasters, captained by Gibson, Whamond and Hopgood, took off on their special strike mission against Gdynia on the night of 26–27 July 1942. When they arrived over their target, they discovered that it was immersed in haze and mist.

Flying over the target for nearly an hour, the aircraft encountered intense flak and only captured slight glimpses of two German warships. The Lancasters performed up to twelve bombing runs and expended all of their weapons. However, none hit their target. Gibson's aircraft missed the target by 400 yards.

Bomber Command's fortune in sinking German warships was later reversed with the advent of another special bomb, the Tallboy. German warships, including the battleships *Bismarck* and *Tirpitz*, battlecruisers *Scharnhorst* and *Gneisenau*, and pocket battleships *Graf Spee*, *Deutschland* (later *Lützow*) and *Admiral von Scheer*, were able to devastate Allied shipping during the early years of the Second World War. However, by 1944 only *Tirpitz*, *Admiral von Scheer* and *Admiral Hipper* continued to serve as viable threats to the Allies.

It was determined by war planners that *Tirpitz* posed the greatest threat to Allied shipping. The German battleship had been ported in a series of Norwegian fjords and maintained the capability to attack Arctic convoys or Allied shipping in the North Atlantic. Bomber Command launched several sorties in vain against the ship. However, by mid-1944, the Tallboy had been developed and the decision was made to use the new weapon against *Tirpitz*.

Due to the long distance between England and the Altafjord, a conventional 'out and return' mission was not considered. Ultimately, the decision was made to launch the sortie, Operation Paravane, from the USSR. The Lancasters were to make their way back to their Soviet base after performing their mission and then return to England. The strike force comprised twenty 617 Squadron Lancasters outfitted with SABS, eighteen 9 Squadron Lancasters equipped with Mk XIV bombsights, a photo-reconnaissance 463 Squadron Lancaster, a PRU Mosquito, and a pair of Liberators transporting spares and groundcrew. Adverse weather and radio beacon compatibility problems caused several aircraft to lose their way en route to the USSR on 11 September. Six Lancasters were put out of commission due to their landing in marshy areas and another returned to England.

Adverse weather continued to plague commencement of the mission. Finally, on 15 September, a strike force of twenty-eight Lancasters was able to take off. When the aircraft arrived over the target area, their aircrews discovered that an immense smokescreen had been laid by the Germans that masked Altafjord. Twenty Lancasters on the mission carried Tallboys, while six or seven carried huge 500lb 'Johnny Walker' mines intended for use against enemy warships in shallow water. A total of seventeen Lancasters managed to drop Tallboys. The remaining bombers returned to the Soviet base of Yagodnik still carrying their Tallboys and 'Johnny Walkers'.

During the raid, one Tallboy struck the *Tirpitz*'s bow and, as a result, the ship sustained significant damage and took on 1,500 tons of water. Other Tallboy near misses inflicted additional damage. Overall damage sustained by the ship from the raid forced the German Navy to regard the *Tirpitz* as unseaworthy for the remainder of the war. Consequently, the Germans made the decision to perform minor repairs on *Tirpitz* and make it a floating coastal defence battery.

Eventually, *Tirpitz* escaped to Tromsø, located closer to Scotland. At Tromsø, the ship was repaired and ultimately moored in the waters off Håkøya island. Thus, Bomber Command made the decision to conduct a second strike on the *Tirpitz* from Scotland. This mission, however, required that the Lancasters be outfitted with auxiliary fuel tanks cannibalised from Wellingtons and Mosquitos. This modification made the Lancasters 2 tons heavier than their conventional weight maximum. Thus, the bombers were lightened by the removal of their front turrets and additional equipment, and given higher-power Merlin 24 engines.

Following 617 Squadron's successful raid on the Dortmund–Ems Canal on 23–24 September 1944 and successful 'dam-busting' attack on the Kembs dam at the Belfort Gap on 7 October, in which Tallboys were used to great effect, Bomber Command commenced preparations for another raid on *Tirpitz*. Nos 9 and 617 Squadron Lancasters were detached to RAF Lossiemouth on

28 October. The next day, twenty Lancasters from each squadron lumbered away toward Tromsø. Unfortunately, the fjord was shrouded in mist by the time the bombers arrived so they dropped thirty-two Tallboys blindly and they badly missed their target. A single Lancaster became a casualty of the mission when it was forced to land in Sweden.

Success against *Tirpitz* was finally achieved on 12 November 1944, when eighteen Lancasters from 617 Squadron and thirteen from 9 Squadron registered three Tallboy hits. After being struck, the ship rolled over. Although the battleship stayed afloat, it was now upside down. The once-feared, mighty *Tirpitz* was now out of commission for the rest of the war.

On 16 April 1945, 617 Lancasters succeeded in sinking the last German pocket battleship, *Lützow*, at Swinemünde. One of the bombers scored a near-miss that ripped open the ship's hull. Consequently, it sank in shallow water. Casualties were light, with only one bomber shot down, while most of the remaining Lancasters sustained light damage from heavy flak.

The capsized *Tirpitz* following a successful strike by 9 and 617 Squadron Lancasters using 12,000lb Tallboy bombs. (Australian military)

Another view of the capsized *Tirpitz*. (WW2images)

11

EFFECTIVE SPECIAL WEAPONS AND COUNTERMEASURES

UPKEEP MINE OR BOUNCING BOMB

In a prelude to Operation Chastise, the assistant chief designer at Vickers-Armstrong, Barnes Wallis, devoted much of his time to the study of dam systems that regulated the river waters serving the Ruhr. These waters yielded drinking water, steel-manufacturing water and hydro-electric power for the Ruhr populace. There were three major dams that were vital to the area: (1) the Eder at Hemfurth, (2) the Möhne at Günne and (3) the Sorpe at Körbecke. Wallis and British war planners reasoned that there was no conventional bomb in the arsenal that possessed the capability of obliterating the huge dams. However, Wallis conceived the idea of exploding a charge under the surface of the water, against the dam, so as to create a shock wave capable of breaching it.

Trials were secretly performed on a dam in Wales that indicated the required explosive amount. With this knowledge in mind, Wallis set out to design a weapon capable of skipping across the surface of the water, gradually decelerating until sinking at a close distance to the dam wall and exploding at a certain depth, set off by a barometric fuse. The weapon was to possess a cylindrical shape and be 'back spun' before being dropped.

Prior to pitching his idea to Bomber Command, Wallis assembled and tested several sub-scale weapon prototypes. Both Wallis and Bomber Command knew that the Lancaster was the only heavy bomber in the arsenal that possessed the capability to carry the full-scale bomb. Wallis estimated that the weapon needed to weigh approximately 9,000lb. Trials with the full-scale weapon, being dropped by a Lancaster, were officially authorised on 28 February 1943. Avro was requested to commence the production of a prototype Lancaster capable of delivering the new weapon to the target. This aircraft became known as the Type 464 Provisioning Lancaster, with the first example serial-numbered ED765/G. Bomber Command also decided to establish a new special squadron to perform these 'dam-busting' missions and Wing Commander Guy Gibson was charged with its formation. Following Gibson's selection of pilots, the unit commenced low-altitude training exercises with no knowledge of its targets. The squadron performed simulated strikes on the Derwent Water dam located in the Peak District.

Dam-busting missions using the bouncing bomb proved to be quite a challenge. The special weapon had to be dropped at an altitude of 60ft above the water and at a speed of 220mph for it to function without detonating upon impact or coming apart. In addition, the bomb had to be released at a precise distance from the dam. A solution to the range accuracy problem was found through the use of a wooden sight with two nails simulating the dam towers: upon their alignment with the actual towers, the Lancaster would be at the correct distance from the dam to release the bomb. Use of the Spotlight Altimeter Calibrator enabled dam-busting Lancaster aircrews to maintain height accuracy during the dam-busting missions.

An order was placed for twenty-three special Lancasters. The new squadron trained for its unique mission using loaned aircraft from the late ED-serial range while its mission-operational aircraft were being converted. The actual Lancasters that would be used were void of dorsal turrets for reduced weight. The bomb doors, bomb racks and related equipment were also removed. Each modified Lancaster had its bomb bay faired over both in the front and rear of the bay to make the aircraft more aerodynamic. The aircraft were also equipped with special mounting arms to accommodate and service the bouncing bombs. These arms were augmented with a motor/belt arrangement that together 'pre-spun' the Upkeep mines at a specific rpm. Each Upkeep mine weighed approximately 9,250lb.

A 617 Squadron Provisioning Lancaster drops an Upkeep mine at Reculver bombing range, Kent. (IWM staff photographers)

The Upkeep mine was tested successfully for the first time on 29 April 1943 by Vickers test pilots 'Mutt' Summers and 'Shorty' Longbottom at Reculver. The feat was achieved following a series of failures in which early mines disintegrated upon water impact. The first successful test was followed by drop testing of inert bouncing bombs at Reculver on 8 May by Gibson and Flight Lieutenants Martin and Hopgood, who led a flight of twelve Provisioning Lancasters loaned to 617 for the test mission. On 13 May 1943, explosive-laden bouncing bombs arrived at Scampton, destined for loading aboard twenty Provisioning Lancasters that were to perform the dam-busting missions.

The effectiveness of the bouncing bomb in combat was previously discussed in Chapter 7.

12,000LB HC BOMB

The 12,000lb HC bomb proved to be an ancient and simple weapon that consisted of a simple three-section cylinder with a tail. The bomb comprised a thin skin, but left much to be desired in the precision department. The need also existed for heavy bombs capable of deeply penetrating targets prior to explosion in such a manner so as to 'shake' immense structures, which caused them to disintegrate.

12,000LB TALLBOY

The 12,000lb Tallboy, conceived by Barnes Wallis, was one of two 'earthquake' bombs and featured a specially designed tail that produced a slight spin upon drop that stopped the bomb from toppling upon achieving compressibility. The Tallboy was capable of achieving a terminal speed of 2,500mph. Construction of the Tallboy proved to be complex and expensive because it was made of steel. The Tallboy's combat debut occurred on 9 June 1944, when 617 Squadron Lancasters released twenty-five of the special weapons against a French railway tunnel at Saumur. The combat effectiveness of the Tallboy was previously discussed in Chapters 8 and 10.

A 4,000lb cookie is prepped for loading aboard 83 Squadron Lancaster L7540 'OL-U' at Wyton. (WW2images)

No. 9 Squadron ground crews move a Tallboy in the bomb dump at Bardney on 9 September 1944. (WW2images)

22,000LB (10-TON) GRAND SLAM

The 22,000lb Grand Slam, also conceived by Barnes Wallis, was the other earthquake bomb and was developed at the same time as the Tallboy. The larger bomb was finally ready for combat by early 1945. A total of thirty-two specially modified Lancaster B.Is (designated B.I (Specials)) were constructed to carry the huge Grand Slam. These featured higher-powered Merlin engines, stronger undercarriage and a modified bomb bay equipped with specially designed bomb restraint/release equipment.

The B.I (Special) prototype, PB592, conducted flight trials alongside the first production variant B.I (Special), PB995, on 1 February 1945. No. 617 Squadron received a pair of B.I (Specials) on 13 March. On that same day, the flight trial aircraft made their initial live drops on the Ashley Walk range in Hampshire.

On 14 March 1945, thirty-two Lancasters and five Mosquitos from 9 and 617 Squadrons successfully attacked the Bielefeld Viaduct. Most of the Lancasters carried Tallboys, but one carried a Grand Slam. The single Grand Slam penetrated deep below the surface and exploded. A couple of the Bielefeld Viaduct's pylons and spans disappeared in the crater. As well, some additional spans that received damage from the Grand Slam were put out of commission by Tallboys released by fourteen other Lancasters from the attacking force. As a result, a 100-yard gap was created in the viaduct.

The Grand Slam was again used to effect later on the Arnsberg Viaduct. This viaduct was vital to the Germans as it connected the main railway system from the Ruhr to Kassel. It was also located halfway between the Möhne and Sorpe dams. Following the aborting of an attack launched on 15 March, five Grand Slams and thirteen Tallboys were eventually dropped on the Arnsberg Viaduct on 19 March. As a result, a 50-yard gap was created in the viaduct and the remaining structure was weakened.

On 22 March, 617 Squadron bombed the Nienburg bridge, located between Bremen and Hanover. One Grand Slam and one Tallboy detonated at each end of the central span and propelled it into the air before it was then struck by another Tallboy. On 23 March, 617 Squadron made its final Grand Slam bridge raid and destroyed a railway bridge at Bremen. Two Grand Slam and two Tallboy strikes were registered during the mission.

The Grand Slam, together with the Tallboy, proved to be quite effective against some German U-boat pens, as demonstrated in 617 Squadron's attack on those at Farge, at the mouth of the Weser, on 27 March. A total of eighteen Lancasters (twelve carrying Grand Slams and six with Tallboys) led the raid, which comprised 100 bombers. A pair of Grand Slams collapsed the roof, while other bombs significantly damaged the remaining structure.

A Lancaster B.I (Special) sporting a revised camouflage scheme and carrying a Grand Slam. (WW2images)

A close-up view of a Grand Slam loaded underneath the fuselage of a Lancaster in 1945. (WW2images)

A Lancaster drops an 11-ton Grand Slam on the viaduct at Arnsberg, Germany, on 19 March 1945. (NARA)

No. 617 Squadron Lancaster B.I (Special) 'YZ-B' in flight above its target, the Arbergen bridge, on 21 March 1945. (WW2images)

'WINDOW' OR 'CHAFF'

In 1943, Bomber Command employed a new revolutionary countermeasure that would change aerial warfare forever. The new device, which became known as 'window' or 'chaff', jammed enemy radar systems. Its development commenced at about the same time that radar was developed. In 1941, window trials began and the perfection of the device was achieved in early 1942. Window's inventor, Welsh physicist-engineer Joan Strothers (Lady Curran), worked in the Radar Countermeasures Group. Strothers conceived a technique that used strips of metal to confuse enemy radar systems. The strips consisted of tinfoil 1 to 2cm in width and 25cm in length that were to be dropped and dispersed from bombers. Window's combat debut occurred during the bombing of Hamburg and resulted in significantly fewer downed British bombers.

Window is released from a Lancaster during a daylight raid on Essen. (WW2images)

12

FINAL MISSIONS OF THE SECOND WORLD WAR

The Lancaster continued to perform vital missions successfully up to the end of the war. On the evening prior to the famous Rhine Crossing of 23 March 1945, seventy-seven 5 Group Lancasters bombed the town of Wesel. In addition, another force of 195 Lancasters also bombed the town that same evening. As a result, Wesel was totally devastated, with all enemy opposition being eliminated.

In April, Lancasters took part in raids against Bayreuth on the 11th; Bremen on the 22nd; Cham on the 17th–18th; Hamburg on the 8th–9th; Harzburg on the 4th–5th; Heligoland on the 18th; Kiel on the 4th–5th, 9th–10th and 13th–14th; Komotau on the 18th–19th; Leipzig on the 10th–11th; Leuna on the 4th–5th; Lützkendorf on the 4th–5th and 8th–9th; Molbis on the 7th–8th; Munich on the 19th; Nordhausen on the 3rd–4th; Nuremberg on the 11th; Pilsen on the 16th–17th; Plauen on the 10th–11th; Potsdam on the 14th–15th; Regensburg on the 20th; and Schwandorf on the 16th–17th.

The 9–10 April raid on Kiel gained remarkable notoriety as during it a strike force of 591 Lancasters achieved saturation bombing of the two primary aim points. The targets were primarily German warships and U-boats, but the bombing caused significant damage to the port infrastructure in addition to sinking eleven ships and two floating docks. Among the German warship casualties were *Admiral Scheer*, *Admiral Hipper* and *Emden*. Only three Lancasters were shot down on the mission.

The Lancaster's final day of combat operations during the war was 25 April 1945. On that day, 617 Squadron bombed the SS barracks at Berchtesgaden with sixteen Tallboys. In addition, a strike force of 158 Lancasters bombed coastal gun batteries on Wangerooge, an island that strategically guarded the approaches to Bremen and Wilhelmshaven. During the raid on Berchtesgaden, fifty-three Lancasters managed to score direct hits on Hitler's Berghof mountain retreat.

The Lancaster's final night of combat operations followed on 25–26 April, when an attacking force of 107 Lancasters and twelve Mosquitos laid waste to an oil refinery at Vallø (Tønsberg), and four Lancasters successfully mined the Oslo fjord.

The final mission flown by the Lancaster during the war was humanitarian in nature. The flights, which became known as Operation Manna, commenced on 29 April, when a force of 3,156 Lancasters and 145 Mosquitos air-dropped food for the beleaguered people of Holland. The two types of bombers together flew approximately 3,298 sorties during the humanitarian operation.

A bomb dropped by a Lancaster explodes near the Berghof on 25 April 1945. (Australian War Memorial)

A Lancaster drops vital food supplies to the Dutch people during Operation Manna. (Unknown photographer)

13

NOSE ART

During the Second World War many Lancasters sported striking art painted onto the forward sections of their fuselages. From 'Glamorous Gals' to highly innovative art designs, Lancaster nose art stood out among Allied heavy bombers. This chapter presents a photographic survey of nose art during the war.

'GLAMOROUS GALS'

Clockwise from top left: A new 463 Squadron RAAF Lancaster 'S for Sugar' at Waddington on 6 December 1944. (Australian War Memorial); Pilot Officer Colin Dickson, 467 Squadron RAAF, poses for a publicity photo in the cockpit of the squadron's Lancaster dubbed 'Naughty Nan' in 1944. (Australian War Memorial); Nose art displayed on 9 Squadron Lancaster 'I'm Easy'. (WW2images)

Opposite: Lancaster NG347 'Princess Pat' in flight. (National Defence Photo Canada, WW2images)

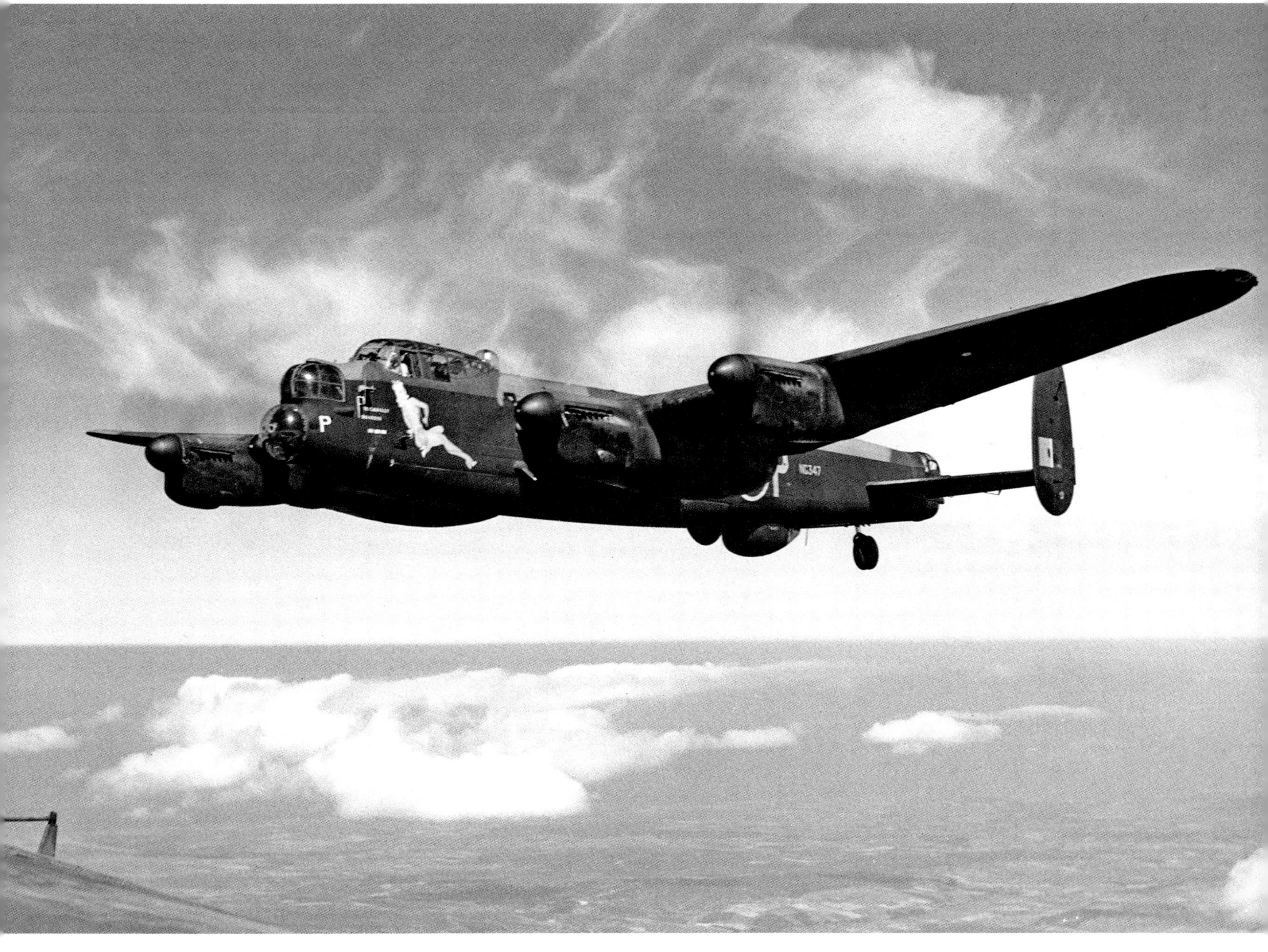

INNOVATIVE ART

Clockwise from top left: No. 460 Squadron RAAF Lancaster 'N for Nuts' at Binbrook on 8 September 1943. The aircraft nose art displays a kangaroo sporting a tartan kilt and carrying a shillelagh, and was intended to represent the Australian, Scottish and Irish crew members of the aircraft. (Australian War Memorial); Ground crew pose by their 463 Squadron RAAF Lancaster at Waddington on 6 December 1944. A mission tally scoreboard is visible ahead of the nose art. (Australian War Memorial); The crew of a 463 Squadron RAAF Lancaster pose for a publicity photo in front of their aircraft at Waddington in July 1944. (Australian War Memorial)

Clockwise from top left: No. 463 Squadron RAAF Lancaster 'Nick the Nazi Neutralizer' at Waddington on 5 December 1944. (Australian War Memorial); A fighting kangaroo and fighting joey in its pouch are displayed in the nose art of 463 Squadron RAAF Lancaster 'X for X-ray' at Waddington on 6 December 1944. The successful completion of twenty-five bombing missions is also marked on the aircraft. (Australian War Memorial); No. 467 Squadron RAAF Lancaster 'P for Peter' at Waddington on 31 August 1943. The nose art displays a kookaburra grasping a snake representing Adolf Hitler. (Australian War Memorial); No. 467 Squadron RAAF Lancaster 'A for Apple' at Waddington on 31 August 1943. (Australian War Memorial)

No. 467 Squadron RAAF Lancaster 'H for Harry' prepares for take-off from Waddington on 31 August 1943. (Australian War Memorial)

Clockwise from above: No. 467 Squadron RAAF Lancaster 'N for Nuts' at Waddington on 6 December 1944. The aircraft's nose art depicts a boxing kangaroo, with a youngster in the pouch 'zamming' Adolf Hitler. (Australian War Memorial); Nose art displayed on 467 Squadron RAAF Lancaster ED547 'PO-M' at Waddington on 31 August 1943. Note the forty bombs, representing the successful completion of forty bombing missions, and an inverted swastika, representative of a German night fighter downed by the crew gunners. (Australian War Memorial); No. 467 Squadron RAAF Lancaster 'R for Robert' at Waddington on 31 August 1943. The aircraft was first known as 'W for Willie' and the nose art depicts King Billy riding a bomb. The spears represent successfully completed bombing missions over enemy territory. (Australian War Memorial)

RAF Lancaster 'Fanny Ferkin II' lands at a USAAF 8th Air Force base in England on 3 May 1944. (NARA)

14

POST-WAR LANCASTERS

The Lancaster's exceptional design and operational career enabled it to serve the RAF and the air forces of other countries well into the post-war era. The type was even adapted for transport use. Following the war, the Lancaster performed several high-profile missions while in RAF service. No. 35 Squadron aircraft performed a public relations tour in America in summer 1946. Some of the aircraft were even autographed by American movie stars. Two Lancasters (PD328 and PB873) successfully completed several long-distance flights, including around the world and trans-polar missions.

The Lancaster continued to serve Bomber Command for several more years before the B.I was replaced by the advanced B.I (F/E) and B.VII (F/E) variants. No. 82 Squadron began receiving new PR.1 photo-reconnaissance Lancasters that sported a silver paint job and were devoid of defensive turrets. Lancaster PR.1s performed aerial surveillance missions of Central and East Africa, with a single PR.1 in operation with the Ministry of Aviation. Some MR.1s, featuring grey paint schemes, served with RAF Coastal Command.

The Lancaster was eventually replaced by the more advanced Avro Lincoln. The last Bomber Command Lancaster was officially retired from service in December 1953. A reconnaissance Lancaster, which was retired in late 1954, had the distinction of being the final aircraft of its type to serve the RAF.

From 1952–53, Avro refurbished fifty-nine Lancaster B.Is and B.VIIs at Woodford and Langar that were pressed into French Aéronavale service. Some of these aircraft flew on until the mid-1960s. They were operated by four squadrons based in France and New Caledonia, performing maritime reconnaissance and search-and-rescue duties.

Fifteen ex-RAF Lancasters were refurbished at Langar and sold to the Argentine Air Force in 1948–49. The Argentine Air Force examples participated in offensive operations aimed at the suppression and support of military coups.

In 1946, modified Lancaster Mk Xs began serving with the RCAF. A total of fourteen of these aircraft saw service in the aerial and photo-reconnaissance roles. These aircraft later performed the majority of the mapping of northern Canada up to 1962. A total of seventy Lancaster 10MR/MPs served with the RCAF in the maritime reconnaissance and patrol roles during the 1950s. The aircraft had radar and sonobuoy operators' positions installed, as well as their rear and mid-upper gun turrets removed. They also featured newly installed 400-gallon fuel tanks in their bomb bays for enhanced range capability and had enhanced electronics, radar, and instrumentation. The RCAF Lancasters remained in service until the end of the 1950s.

After the Second World War, Lancasters performed a variety of transport missions, most notably the transport of thousands of PoWs in Europe back to England. Both soldiers and PoWs were transported by these aircraft until November 1945.

In 1946, civil transport variants of the Lancaster began to see use as freighters. Four such aircraft saw service with British South American Airways, but they served for only a year because they were uneconomical. Four Lancaster IIIs underwent conversion by Flight Refuelling Limited into a pair of tankers and a pair of receiver aircraft slated for in-flight refuelling development duty.

A converted long-distance transport Lancaster Mark X variant was pressed into transatlantic military passenger and postal delivery service by the Canadian Government Trans-Atlantic Air Service (CGTAS) in 1943–47. A total of nine of these aircraft, designated as Lancaster XPPs, were built. In 1947, the CGTAS was absorbed into Trans-Canada Air Lines. The Lancaster XPPs then transported civilian passengers, who paid to fly on them. The aircraft were eventually replaced by Douglas DC-4s in 1947.

No. 35 Squadron RAF Lancasters in flight over English fields in 1946. No. 35 Squadron, also known as the 'RAF's Famous Thirty-Five', achieved notoriety during the war for taking part in numerous night-bombing missions over Germany, devastating the war industry. During the latter part of the war, the squadron was slated for duty in the Pacific against Japan as part of the Tiger Force but VJ-Day came before they saw any action. (NARA)

A RAF photographic reconnaissance squadron Lancaster lands at RAF Canal Zone Station following the completion of a flight from East Africa in 1953. (NARA)

One of the last Lancasters in RAF service, with Coastal Command, in 1955. (NARA)

The last Lancaster in RAF service, with Coastal Command, in flight in 1956. (NARA)

A 407(MR) Squadron RCAF Lancaster Mk 10MP. (San Diego Air and Space Museum Archives)

No. 405 Squadron RCAF Lancaster Mk 10MPs at Naval Air Station Jacksonville, Florida, in February 1953. No. 405 Squadron served as a maritime patrol squadron and was stationed at Greenwood, Nova Scotia, Canada. (USN)

AVRO LANCASTRIAN

A further civil development of the Lancaster appeared in the form of the Avro Lancastrian. Victory Aircraft of Canada completed the conversion of a Lancaster X bomber into a civil transport in 1943, slating the aircraft for service with Trans-Canada Airlines (TCA). After the war, Victory Aircraft became a part of Avro Canada. The conversion proved to be so successful that eight more Lancaster Xs were converted. These aircraft featured Merlin 38 engines as well as extended, more aerodynamic noses and tail cones. The addition of two 400-gallon Lancaster long-range fuel tanks to their bomb bays enabled the aircraft to fly with a much greater distances. The initial Lancastrians saw service with TCA flying the Montreal–Prestwick route.

A total of thirty British-constructed Lancastrians saw service with BOAC in 1945. To demonstrate the capabilities of the Lancastrian, G-AGLF flew 13,500 miles from England to Auckland, New Zealand, in three days, fourteen hours from 23 to 26 April 1945. The top speed was 220mph.

The Lancastrian proved to be swift and could fly with a great range. The aircraft could also transport heavy loads. Interior space, however, proved to be limited. The Lancastrian was not capable of carrying a great number of passengers, but was better suited to carrying mail and a few VIP passengers. Beginning on 31 May 1945, BOAC Lancastrians began flying routes from England to Australia.

Lancastrians saw service with the RAF, Qantas and Flota Aérea Mercante Argentina. They were also effectively utilised during the Berlin Airlift. A total of fifteen aircraft performed in excess of 5,000 flights, successfully delivering vital petrol to beleaguered Berliners. A BSAA Lancastrian had the distinction of being the first aircraft to operate a scheduled flight from London Heathrow Airport in 1946. A total of ninety-one Lancastrians were produced and some remained in service until 1960.

The Lancastrian (Lancaster I PD328) *Aries* performs a trans-polar flight mission in 1945. (NARA)

Another view of *Aries* during the same mission. (NARA)

THE LANCASTRIAN AS AN ENGINE TESTBED

The development and emergence of the gas turbine (turbojet) engine in the aviation world brought the need to flight test the new technology on a testbed aircraft. Subsequently, the Lancastrian was seen to fit the bill and several saw service with Rolls-Royce. Turbojet engines replaced the outer engines, while test piston engines could replace the Merlins in the inner nacelles.

A static view of a Lancastrian turbojet engine testbed in 1947. (NARA)

A rear view of the testbed. (NARA)

A frontal view of a Lancastrian turbojet engine testbed at Villacoublay Aerodrome, France, on 18 November 1946. (NARA)

Side view of the same aircraft at the same location. (NARA)

A Lancastrian turbojet engine testbed in flight on 2 September 1947. (NARA)

15

SURVIVORS

Today, there are a total of seventeen Lancaster survivors in existence. Only two are capable of flight: (1) PA474, stationed at Coningsby in Lincolnshire, England, is routinely flown by the Battle of Britain Memorial Flight and (2) VR-A FM213 *Vera* resides in Canada and is flown by the Canadian Warplane Heritage Museum in Mount Hope, Ontario. Lancaster B.VII NX611 *Just Jane* is preserved at the East Kirkby Lincolnshire Aviation Heritage Centre and is capable of taxiing but is not currently flight capable. The refurbished B.X FM159 is at the Bomber Command Museum of Canada in Nanton, Alberta.

An airworthy Lancaster survivor, RAF Lancaster B.I PA474 performs a demonstration flight during Air Fete '88 at RAF Mildenhall, Suffolk, on 28 May 1988. (NARA)

SUMMARY

During the Second World War, the Lancaster served as the ultimate strategic asset for Britain. From the initial risky daylight bombing missions over Europe to the fire-bombing of German cities, the Dambuster raids, the bombing of Peenemünde and the sinking of the *Tirpitz*, the Lancaster helped to secure victory for the Allies. Furthermore, the aircraft proved to be effective in strategic precision bombing of targets such as enemy troop concentrations, railways, aqueducts and V-1 flying-bomb launch sites. The combat effectiveness of the Lancaster in the Second World War remains unquestioned. As stated by Adolf Galland, commander of the Luftwaffe's fighters, after the war, the Lancaster was 'the best night bomber of the war'.[1] Arthur Harris also later proclaimed the Lancaster to have been Bomber Command's 'shining sword'.[2]

LANCASTER VERSUS THE AMERICANS

The Lancaster compared favourably to other Allied heavy bombers during the war. It possessed a great range capability, similar to the USAAF Consolidated B-24 Liberator and greater than the Boeing B-17 Flying Fortress. The Lancaster was also capable of carrying more bombs than both of its American contemporaries, and furthermore it possessed the ability to serve as a special weapons carrier, modified to carry the bouncing, Tallboy and Grand Slam bombs.

Following the war, the Lancaster remained in service with the air forces of several countries, for some until the mid-1960s. Civil variants of the Lancaster served with distinction as a transport. Thus, the Avro Lancaster remains an iconic Second World War heavy bomber legend in aviation history.

NOTES

Chapter 2: Design and Development

1 RG 255, NACA Classified File 1915–58, 1105.4 Army GA/1 thru 1105.4 Avro Lancaster 3/10, Box 455, 1105.4-Avro Lancaster/1, Air Fighting Development Unit Report No. 47 on Tactical Trials – Lancaster Aircraft, Wing Commander, Commanding, AFDU, 30 May 1942, p.1. US National Archives at College Park, Maryland, Textual Reference Branch.
2 Ibid., p.3.
3 Ibid., p.6.
4 Goulding, Brian, and Garbett, M., *The Avro Lancaster I: Aircraft in Profile Number 65* (Leatherhead, Surrey: Profile Publications, 1966), p.3.

Chapter 4: Bombing German Cities

1 Partworks Ltd, *Lancaster: The Backbone of Bomber Command* (UK: Hachette Partworks Ltd, 2019), p.47.
2 Harris, Sir Arthur, *Bomber Offensive* (London: Greenhill Books, 2005), p.52. The Old Testament of the Holy Bible – Hosea 8:7, bible.oremus.org/?passage =hosea8:7&version=nrsv.

Chapter 16: Summary

1 Galland, Adolf, *The First and the Last: Germany's Fighter Force in WWII* (*Fortunes of War*) (Black Hawk, Colorado: Cerberus Press, 2005), p.119.
2 Iveson, Tony, *Lancaster: The Biography* (London: Andre Deutsch Ltd, 2009), p.82.

BIBLIOGRAPHY

Galland, Adolf, *The First and the Last: Germany's Fighter Force in WWII* (*Fortunes of War*) (Black Hawk, Colorado: Cerberus Press, 2005).

Goulding, Brian, and Garbett, M., *The Avro Lancaster I: Aircraft in Profile Number 65* (Leatherhead, Surrey: Profile Publications, 1966).

Hachette Partworks Ltd, *Lancaster: The Backbone of Bomber Command* (UK: Hachette Partworks Ltd, 2019).

Harris, Sir Arthur, *Bomber Offensive* (London: Greenhill Books, 2005).

Iveson, Tony, *Lancaster: The Biography* (London: Andre Deutsch Ltd, 2009).

Lake, Jon, *Lancaster Squadrons: 1942–43* (Oxford: Osprey Publishing, 2002).

Lake, Jon, *Lancaster Squadrons: 1944–45* (Oxford: Osprey Publishing, 2002).

RG 255, NACA Classified File 1915–58, 1105.4 Army GA/1 thru 1105.4 Avro Lancaster 3/10, Box 455, 1105.4-Avro Lancaster/1, Air Fighting Development Unit Report No. 47 on Tactical Trials – Lancaster Aircraft, Wing Commander, Commanding, AFDU, 30 May 1942. US National Archives at College Park, Maryland, Textual Reference Branch.

The History Press
The destination for history
www.thehistorypress.co.uk